The 12 Tribes of Israel

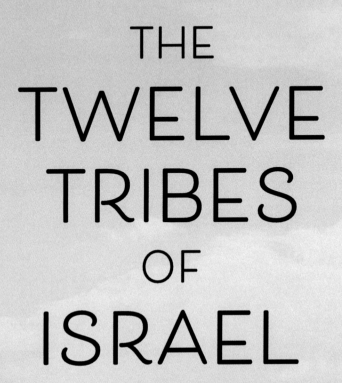

THE TWELVE TRIBES OF ISRAEL

AN ARTISTIC & HISTORICAL JOURNEY

ERIC M. DOROSHOW
ARTIST · AUTHOR · ATTORNEY

The Twelve Tribes of Israel:
An Artistic & Historical Journey

All Watercolor Artwork
Eric Doroshow by

Paintings by Eric Doroshow

ISBN: 978-0-578-65969-5

Library of Congress Control Number: 2020907534

Weldin Park Associates LLC
1202 Kirkwood Highway
Wilmington, DE 19805

Israel Photographs Courtesy of Unsplash:
Resul © 2018
Daniel Straub © 2018
Damian Denis © 2018
Yanny Mishchuk © 2019
Heather Shevlin © 2016
Chris Gallimore © 2016
Benjamin Grull © 2018
Aviv Ben © 2017
Akhil Lincoln © 2019
Tim De Groot © 2013
Dave Herring © 2019
Zoltan Tasi © 2018
Emile Guillemot © 2019
Alex Azabache © 2019
Sammy Leigh © 2016
Lee Miller © 2015

CONTENTS

INTRODUCTION

THE INSPIRATION FOR THIS PAINTING AND
BOOK ABOUT THE 12 TRIBES OF ANCIENT ISRAEL
BEGAN IN NOVEMBER 2016, WHEN MY WIFE,
AIDA, SEVERAL OTHER FRIENDS AND I WERE
ON A TRIP TO ISRAEL.

On a cloudless day our bus pulled up to Kibbutz
Lotan, which seemed to be little more than a spot
of green in the otherwise stark, foreboding, almost
moonlike Arava Valley in the Negev desert.

Our plan was to meet with Rabbi Daniel Burstyn,
who is a member of the Kibbutz. We were familiar
with the Rabbi because for several years he helped
lead our congregation at High Holiday services at
Seaside Jewish Community in Rehoboth Beach,
Delaware.

During the first night there, we learned from
Rabbi Daniel that Kibbutz Lotan is based on profit
sharing and egalitarian Jewish values. We got a
first-hand presentation about Eco-living and how

it literally made the desert bloom at the Kibbutz.

The next morning, most of our group was off to tour Petra, Jordan, but I stayed behind with a couple of friends to paint, hike and contemplate. I began thinking about the 12 Tribes of Ancient Israel and how they must have passed through the Arava Valley Desert, the very area where I stood.

Earlier in the trip, we had seen The Chagall windows at the Hadassah Medical Center at Ein Karem, Jerusalem, which also provided inspiration for these paintings.

Upon my return home, I began my research about the tribes. I learned that each tribe had a flag, a symbol and a color. My primary research sources for the paintings and the book were taken from the Holy Scriptures of the Tanakh, The Encyclopedia Judaica (1972 edition), Hadassah Hospital's website on the Chagall paintings, www.hadassah-medical.com and The Jerusalem Windows of Marc Chagall by Jean Leymarie.

After completing my research, I began Part One of this project. I painted 12 watercolors, each representing a tribe. I picked the symbols and the colors I felt best described the essence of each tribe.

After completing the 12 watercolors, I then began working with a local artist for ideas about how to display the paintings as a group that would become a professionally prepared giclée print on archival paper.

However, I felt that I had to do more than just paint. I needed to write a book to explain the paintings and provide more information about each tribe. I therefore began part two of this task: a book about the 12 tribes. This book is not intended to be a full-blown religious or historical survey. Its purpose is to share with you, the reader, what I learned about each tribe, thus giving you a better understanding of the paintings.

In the book, I quote some relevant sections of the Bible and other religious scriptures that discuss the tribes. You will see quotes from the Midrash[1] and

---

1 This is not the Bible but a compilation of Rabbinic literature and commentary on the Bible.

from the Aggadah[2]. Much of what I have written originated with the research from *The Encyclopedia Judaica* (1972 Edition), The Jewish Virtual Library, and Hadassah Hospital's website on the Chagall paintings: http://www.hadassah-med.com/about/art-at-hadassah/chagall-windows.aspx

So, let's begin our artistic and historic journey together as we learn about the 12 Tribes of Israel. For the benefit of the reader, there is space for notes at the end of every chapter.

2 The Aggadah is a compilation of folklore, comments of Rabbis and stories interpreting the Jewish Bible.

1441   9780578659695   1441

Location: ZK-13

ZBM.PNQ7

Title:	The 12 Tribes of Israel: An Artistic & Historical Journey
Cond:	Very Good
User:	zbk_list
Station:	ZBK07
Date:	2023-03-29 14:04:25 (UTC)
Account:	ZBK Books
Orig Loc:	ZK-13
mSKU:	ZBM.PNQ7
Seq#:	1441
unit_id:	8263822
width:	0.25 in
rank:	2,320,746
Source:	GRISELDA

delist unit# 8263822

xxxxx

A SHORT HISTORY OF THE 12 TRIBES OF ISRAEL

THE STORY OF THE 12 TRIBES OF ISRAEL, COL-LECTIVELY CALLED ISRAEL, IS TOLD IN DETAIL IN THE BIBLE[1]. THE PEOPLE WHO WERE TO MAKE UP THE 12 TRIBES LEFT EGYPT TO AVOID BURDENSOME LABOR UNDER THE PHARAOH.

According to the Book of Exodus 12:37: Moses left Egypt with 600,000 men on foot, besides women and children. God rescued the Israelites from Egyptian oppression and helped keep them alive in the desert. At Sinai, they received the laws and regulations and made a covenant to God. Under the leadership of Moses, they wandered for 40 years in the desert before they reached Canaan. Joshua led them into the land of Canaan, which was to become the land of ancient Israel.

---

1 The story of the 12 Ancient Tribes of Israel is told in the Holy Scriptures of the Jewish bible. The story was first told in the Pentateuch also called the Torah. These five books are: Genesis, Exodus, Leviticus, Numbers and Deuteronomy. The story is also told in the Tanakh and the Holy Scriptures which consists of eight books of the prophets and eleven books of additional writings.

The Israelites were traditionally divided into 12 tribes. Biblical tradition holds that the tribes are descended from the sons and grandsons of Jacob.

God made Himself known to Moses and rescued the Israelites from an oppressive pharaoh in Egypt. At Mt. Sinai, the nation received its laws and made a Covenant with God. The 12 tribes were blessed by Jacob and Moses in Genesis and Deuteronomy. According to the commentary by Jean Leymarie in *"The Jerusalem Windows"*:

> *Jacob called to his side his 12 sons (who gave their names to the 12 tribes) and blessed each, calling each by name and revealing his nature and destiny....*

> *The dying Moses repeated Jacob's solemn act and in a somewhat different order, also blessed the 12 tribes of Israel who were about to enter the land of Canaan.*

The 12 tribes were Asher, Benjamin, Dan, Gad, Issachar, Joseph, Judah, Levi, Naphtali, Reuben, Simeon and Zebulun.

Modern scholarship is conflicted about much of the history of the tribes. Nevertheless, it appears that their covenant with the one God of Israel,

their common history and religion, bound them together.

Each tribe was made up of several clans, although the tribe of Dan supposedly consisted of a single clan. The Tabernacle[2] and the Ark of the Covenant[3] were the most sacred religious objects of the tribal union and they were in Shiloh (Joshua 18:1).

Shiloh was the center of worship for the tribes and was in the mountain of the territory of Ephraim. It was here that the tribes also assembled to settle intertribal disputes. Lots were cast for the various tribal areas. However, the tribe of Levi received no land, as "the priesthood of the LORD is their portion." (Joshua 18:1)

The war against Nahash the Ammonite showed that the tribes came to their mutual military aid if any one of the tribes had difficulty.[4] In one case,

2 Also called the Tent of Meeting, it was the portable sanctuary constructed by the Children of Israel while wandering in the desert. Its construction was done at the command of God. (Exodus 39:32). It was the place where the Divine Presence was revealed and where a cloud of the Lord appeared. (Exodus 40:34).

3 A gold-covered wooden chest with lid covered described in the Book of Exodus as containing the 10 Commandments.

4 King Nahash tried to subjugate a Israelite city named Jaabesh-Gilead. The inhabitants appealed to King Saul who assembled and army of Israel and routed the Ammonites (1 Samuel 11). Saul's

unified action by the tribes was started against the Tribe of Benjamin for a breach of the terms of the covenant.

The War of Deborah (Judges 4) gives clear evidence that there was some coordination of military efforts among the tribes. In the Song of Deborah (Judges 5), the battle was recounted in a poem. The leading warriors and tribes were praised, while other tribes that did not participate were mocked. Praiseworthy were the tribes of Ephraim, Benjamin, Manasseh, Zebulun, Issachar and Naphtali. Discredited were the tribes of Reuben, Gad, Dan and Asher. Judah and Simeon were not mentioned.

Some of the tribes worked together. For example, the tribe of Zebulun engaged in trade and supported the tribe of Issachar. This was done to enable the members of Issachar to devote themselves to the study of the Torah. All of the tribes produced judges, kings and prophets, except for Simeon.

handling of this crisis showed his capacity of leadership. Interestingly, he later showed kindness to King David. (II Samuel 10:2).

The number 12 was considered sacred, governing heaven and earth. In addition to the 12 tribes of ancient Israel, there were 12 gates of Jerusalem and there were 12 carved gems in Aaron's breastplate. It is recorded that Joshua was told by the Lord to pick up 12 stones from the Jordan River, corresponding to the number of tribes and that a member of each tribe took one stone as a memorial of the crossing into Jordan (Joshua 4:7).

The tribe of Levi did not receive any land. When Levi is counted among the 12 tribes, the Joseph tribes are counted as one. However, when Levi is not mentioned, the Joseph tribe is split in two between Joseph's sons and counted separately as Manasseh and Ephraim.

Each tribe had a flag of a different color, corresponding to the stone on Aaron's breastplate.

Under the leadership of Joshua, they united and conquered the land of Canaan, which was then divided among them.

Between the death of Joshua and the institution

of Kings in ancient Israel, judges[5] and elders of each tribe wielded political and judicial authority. Each tribe maintained a good deal of autonomy and there was no predetermined method of leadership among the tribes. As we shall see later in this book, the tribes occasionally cooperated in joint military actions against a common foe, and some common administrative duties were shared among them.

Under the impact of military pressures, the tribes were compelled to turn to Samuel to establish a monarchy, and Saul was crowned to rule over all the tribes. (I Samuel 11:15).

It was in the service of King Saul that David began his career to assume the throne. He had a close relationship with the tribe of Judah through marriage and through gifts he made to notables of Judah.

The elders of Israel went to Hebron and "King David made a covenant with them at Hebron before the Lord, and they anointed David King

5 They were not Judges in the legal sense as we know them. They were charismatic leaders who led single tribes or groups of tribes. Their Rule was temporary, and they did not receive the allegiance of all the tribes.

over Israel" (II Samuel 5:3). Thus, at the age of 30, he became King of both Judah and Israel. He made Jerusalem ancient Israel's capital city, from which he administered the State. David ruled over all 12 tribes in a united monarchy. He eventually consolidated the tribes into a territorial entity, but by doing so weakened their tribal consciousness.

After the death of David, the tribes once again split along territorial and political lines. Judah and Benjamin in the south were loyal to the house of David. The tribes of the north were loyal to a succession of monarchies. The new northern kingdom, consisting of 10 tribes, adopted the name Israel, while the southern kingdom took the name Judah.

Israel's capital became Samaria, and its religious centers were Bethel and Dan. The capital of Judah and its religious center was Jerusalem.

THE LEGEND OF THE 10 LOST TRIBES

WITHOUT QUESTION, THE LEGEND OF THE FATE OF THE "10 LOST TRIBES", WHICH CONSISTED OF THE 10 TRIBES OF THE NORTHERN KINGDOM OF ISRAEL, IS ONE OF THE MOST FASCINATING STORIES IN JUDAISM.

The northern kingdom of Israel remained autonomous until it was eventually defeated by the Assyrians in the year 722 B.C.E. In II Kings 17:6 and 18:11, we read that the inhabitants of these tribes were exiled to Halah and Harbor by the river Gozan in Assyria. We are told that this happened because they did not obey the Lord their God, by not obeying and fulfilling His covenant.

The Assyrian army had advanced weapons for its time. They were brutal in their conquest of their enemies. Forced removal of conquered populations was their practice. This is the likely the fate of the 10 northern tribes once they were defeated by the Assyrians.

After their forced removal, some believed that the tribes disappeared from history, lost forever, never to return. This was the view of Rabbi Akiva.

However, there were prophesies that the tribes would continue to maintain a separate existence and that, in time, they would join with their brethren. See I Chronicles 5:26, where it is written that the 10 tribes remained "to this day". Some believed this passage, as well as the prophecies of Isaiah 11:15 and Jeremiah 31:8. This kept alive the belief in re-unification. In Ezekiel 37:21-22, it is also written that God will take the Israelite people "from among the nations they have gone to... and bring them to their own land." One King, it is said, will rule over the entire nation, never permitting a division into two kingdoms again.

According to *The Encyclopedia Judaica*, during the period of the Second Temple and of the Talmud, the belief in the continuing existence of the 10 tribes was regarded as absolutely true. The continued existence of the tribes also appears to find support in writings of Josephus, Ezra, Paul and

James in the New Testament.

Throughout the ages, even to modern times, there were claims of the existence of the 10 lost tribes by both scholars and travelers, both Jewish and non Jewish, in virtually all parts of the world.

There is a fascinating story about a man named Eldad the Danite. In 883 C.E,, the Jewish community in Spain received a letter from the Jewish community in Tunisia describing a visit from Eldad who spoke to them only in Hebrew at a time when Hebrew was not a conversational language. He claimed to have traveled extensively. He gave a very detailed account of each of the lost tribes and their whereabouts. He said he was a member of the tribe of Dan and communicated with members of the tribes of Dan, Naphtali, Gad and Asher.

Eldad said that he arrived in an area in the mountains around modern day Iran where he found a member of the lost tribe of Issachar. He said that Reuben and Zebulun were neighbors in the mountains. They were in what is modern day Turkey. The tribes of Ephraim and western Manasseh lived in an area that is today Yemen and southern

Saudi Arabia.

Another fascinating story concerns Antonio Levi de Montezinos, who returned to Amsterdam from South America in 1644. He told of having found Indians in the mountains who greeted him by reciting the Shema.

More recently, compelling stories continue to appear about the lost tribes. According to the book *The Rebbe's Army* by Sue Fishkoff (2003), members of the Church of Jesus Christ of Latter-day Saints consider themselves to be descended from the lost tribe of Ephraim. The church's major building is called the Temple, and its assembly hall has a large Star of David.

In *My Father's Paradise: A Son's Search for His Jewish Past in Kurdish Iraq*, Ariel Sabar wrote in 2008 about his father growing up in a thriving Jewish community in a remote and isolated Kurdish region of northern Iraq. For centuries, Jews lived in isolated villages in the mountains, cut off from civilization and largely cut off from one another. They spoke the ancient tongue of Aramaic. They were largely illiterate, left behind few written records and had no printing press. They toiled at backbreaking jobs and were beholden to warring tribal chieftains. They lived as small minorities across the Kurdish regions of Iraq, Syria, Iran and Turkey. Sabar believes that they lived in the land area where the Assyrians "pushed them" 2700 years before. Their major accomplishment was their survival.

Sabar writes on page 54:

> *"Over the years, Jewish enclaves as far flung as China, India, Venezuela, and Ethiopia have asserted ancestry in the Lost Tribes. But the Jews of Kurdistan might be said to have the strongest claim. For better and worse, they stayed right where the Assyrians had put them. They had not perished. They were not even lost. They were just too far outside the beltway for anyone to notice."*

In the 1950s, this community of 120,000 Jews escaped to Israel and started a new life there.

NOTES

_____

_____

_____

_____

_____

_____

_____

_____

_____

_____

_____

_____

_____

_____

_____

_____

_____

_____

_____

_____

_____

_____

_____

_____

THE TRIBE OF ASHER

ASHER WAS JACOB'S EIGHTH SON, SECOND SON OF ZILPAH, LEAH'S SERVANT. ASHER IS A FULL BROTHER TO GAD AND WAS BLESSED WITH RICHES. THE NAME ASHER MEANS "PRAISE".

The tribe of Asher settled in northwest Canaan along the Mediterranean Sea on some of the most fertile land in the area. The Bible references to the tribe are replete with references to the fertility of the land (Genesis 49:20). Its principal cultivation was the olive tree, a symbol of opulence and joy. In the Aggadah, it is written that the land of Asher was so fertile that it supplied all of Israel's agricultural needs, including olives.

The tribe developed in tranquility, but this may have taken away the tribe's incentive for national leadership. Asher was the only tribe not to have a national spokesman in the period of the Judges.

Asher did not participate in some battles. In fact, the tribe was criticized by Deborah for not participating in an important battle (Judges 5:17).

At the beginning of the second decade of David's reign, the tribe developed a close relationship with the Kingdom of David. Four cities from Asher were given to the Levites. The kings of Judah attempted to extend their rule over Asher (II Chronicles 30:10-12).

Asher is symbolized in my painting by the olive branch as reflected in the blessings of Moses. The aquamarine color in the background symbolizes the tribe's color as suggested in the Midrash.

NOTES

_____
_____
_____
_____
_____
_____
_____
_____
_____
_____

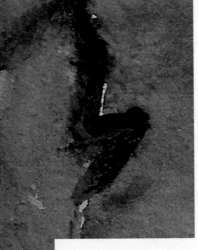

Jacob's blessing, Genesis 49

"Benjamin is a ravenous wolf;
In the morning he will consume the foe;
And in the evening he will divide the spoil."

Moses' blessing, Deuteronomy 33

"Beloved of the LORD,
He rests securely beside Him;
Ever does He protect him
As He dwells amid his slopes."

Midrash Rabbah Bamidbar 2

"His gem was jasper (YASHPE),
his color was a mixture of all colors.
His emblem was a ravening wolf."

THE TRIBE OF BENJAMIN

BENJAMIN WAS THE YOUNGEST SON OF JACOB AND RACHEL, WHO DIED IN CHILDBIRTH. THE TRIBE'S TERRITORY WAS SPREAD OUT BETWEEN THE HILL COUNTRY OF EPHRAIM TO THE HILL COUNTRY OF JUDAH AND AS FAR AS THE DEAD SEA. THE TRIBE'S SOUTHERN BORDER WAS THE NORTHERN BORDER OF JUDAH (JOSHUA 15:5-11). THE TRIBE'S TERRITORY WAS OF STRATEGIC IMPORTANCE AS MAIN ROADS RAN NORTH-SOUTH AND ALSO WEST THROUGH ITS TERRITORY.

The members of the tribe of Benjamin were proven warriors (Judges 9-21). This is expressed in Jacob's blessing as stated above. In the days of Deborah, Benjamin joined in fighting Jabin and Sisera (Judges 5:14). The tribe was central in fighting the Philistines.

Although Jerusalem formally belonged to no tribe, the Temple Mount is situated in the territory of

Benjamin. This might explain the blessing of Moses in the previous page.

Benjamin was considered a small tribe, but it played a major role in the unification of the 12 tribes during the period of the Judges and the beginning of the monarchy. From the tribe of Benjamin came the first king of Israel, Saul.

The tribe was almost wiped out by the other tribes in the intertribal war that followed the affair of the concubine of Gibeah. Benjamin was defeated and most of its civilian population was wiped out. In fact, the tribe only survived because women in Jabesh-Gilend and Shiloh were seized as potential wives for 600 of the remaining unmarried warriors (Judges 21).

When David became king, the tribe retained some of its rancor against David because he supplanted the house of Saul (II Samuel 16:5-13). Benjamin became an administrative district under David and Solomon (I Kings 4:18).

In my watercolor, the ferocity of the tribe reflected in Jacob's blessing is shown by the howling wolf.

The red jasper color of the tribe as suggested in the Midrash is shown in the background.

NOTES
_____
_____
_____
_____
_____
_____
_____
_____
_____
_____
_____
_____
_____
_____
_____
_____
_____
_____
_____

Jacob's blessing, Genesis 49

"Dan shall govern his people
as one of the tribes of Israel.
Dan shall be a serpent by the road,
A viper by the path,
That bites the horses' heels
So the rider is thrown back."

Midrash Rabbah Bamidbar 2

"His gem was zircon (LESHEM),
and his flag was sapphire-like, with
a serpent drawn on it, as it is written:
Dan will be as a serpent on a road."

THE TRIBE OF DAN

DAN WAS THE FIRST CHILD OF BILHAH, RACHAEL'S SERVANT (GENESIS 30:6). ITS BROTHER TRIBE WAS NAPHTALI. THE TRIBE OF DAN HAD A VERY DIFFICULT HISTORY. IT STRUGGLED FOR RECOGNITION IN THE CONFEDERATION, AND ALSO STRUGGLED FOR ITS SURVIVAL AGAINST NOMADIC TRIBES AND THE PHILISTINES.

There was a rivalry between the tribes of Dan and Judah on religious matters including the path toward monotheism.

Its original territory was between Ephraim and Judah, which included a coastal strip around the famous port of Jaffa. But the Amorites drove the tribe back from this land. In Judges 18, the tribe's efforts to find new territory in the northeast region of Palestine are recounted in detail. The operation to find a new home began with spies to explore the land. After that, the conquest of the city of

Laish was undertaken, but it presented no great military problems.

The territory of Dan was considered the northern flank of the Kingdom of Israel and the tribe suffered mightily in wars against Aram and Assyria.

In the Song of Deborah, the tribe was criticized for not joining together with the other tribes to fight the Canaanites. In Judges 5:17, it is asked, "why did they linger by the ships?"

Recent archeological findings as reported in the October 30, 2018 issue of Haaretz suggests that the Danites worshiped Yahweh as their main deity. However, King Jeroboam of Dan pushed the tribe to idolatry.

During the time of David, the tribal territories of Dan were consolidated and made into an administrative unit.

The tribe was eventually conquered by Tiglath-Pileser III in 732 B.C.E. and its inhabitants were exiled to Assyria (II Kings 15:29).

Some scholars believe that the Jews of Ethiopia

were direct descendants of the Tribe of Dan.

In my watercolor, I painted a serpent by a road, posed to bite, as reflected in Jacob's Blessing. The blue sapphire color of the tribe as suggested in the Midrash is surrounding the serpent.

NOTES

_____

_____

_____

_____

_____

_____

_____

_____

_____

_____

_____

_____

_____

_____

_____

_____

27

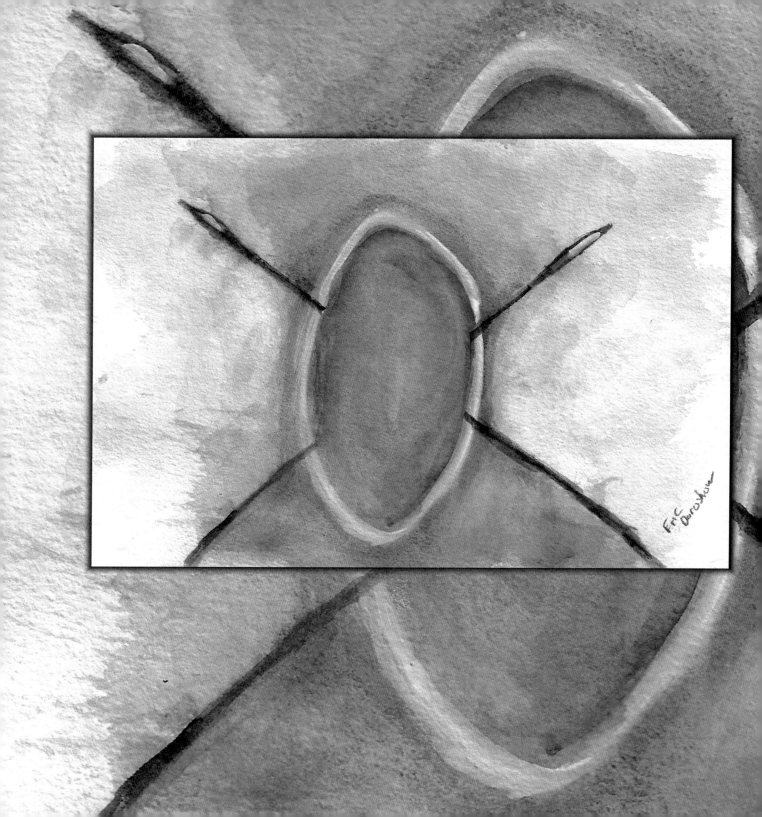

Jacob's blessing, Genesis 49

"Gad shall be raided by raiders,
But he shall raid at their heels."

Moses' blessing, Deuteronomy 33

"Blessed be HE who enlarges Gad!
Poised is he like a lion
To tear off arm and scalp.
He chose for himself the best,
For there is a portion of revered chieftain,
Where the heads of the people come.
He carried out the LORD's judgments
And HIS decisions for Israel"

Midrash Rabbah Bamidbar 2

"His gem was agate (SHVA),
and his flag was neither white nor black,
but a mixture thereof.
There was a military camp drawn on it,
as it is written:
Gad shall be raided by raiders."

THE TRIBE OF GAD

GAD WAS THE FIRST SON OF ZILPAH, LEAH'S SERVANT. THE TRIBE RECEIVED THE LAND OF TRANSJORDAN, BETWEEN REUBEN AND MANASSEH, OF WHICH THEY TOOK POSSESSION AFTER HELPING THE OTHER TRIBES CONQUER THE LAND OF CANNAN.

Gadites were famous warriors. The history of Gad is a history of a succession of wars with its neighbors and nomadic tribes. They were considered men of might, who could handle shield and buckler, whose faces were like lions and who were as swift as gazelles upon the mountains (I Chronicles 5:18).

Gad supported David in his wars against Aram, Ammon and Moab. Elijah the prophet was a native of Gad.

The tribe of Gad entered into a military and fraternal alliance with Benjamin (Judges 21). There were ties between Gad and Judah during the reign of Jotham (I Chronicles 5:17).

In 732 B.C.E., the tribe was invaded by Tiglath Pileser III and most of the inhabitants were exiled (II Kings 15:2).

The warlike nature of the tribe as reflected in Jacob's blessing is depicted in the painting of the shield. The Midrash indicates that the flag color was neither black, nor white, but a mixture, and this is shown in the background of the painting.

NOTES
_____
_____
_____
_____
_____
_____
_____
_____
_____
_____
_____

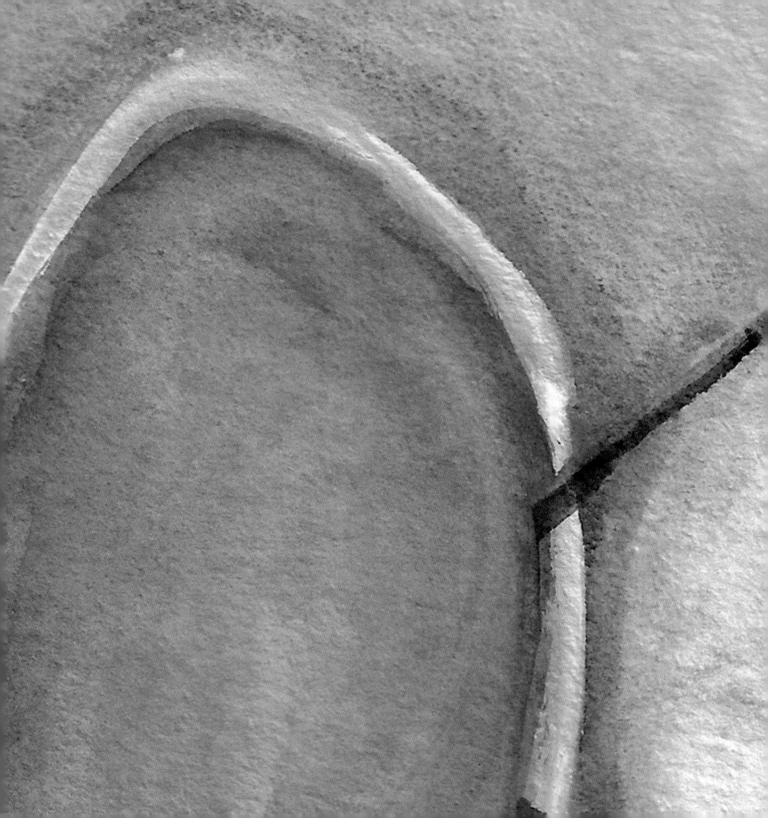

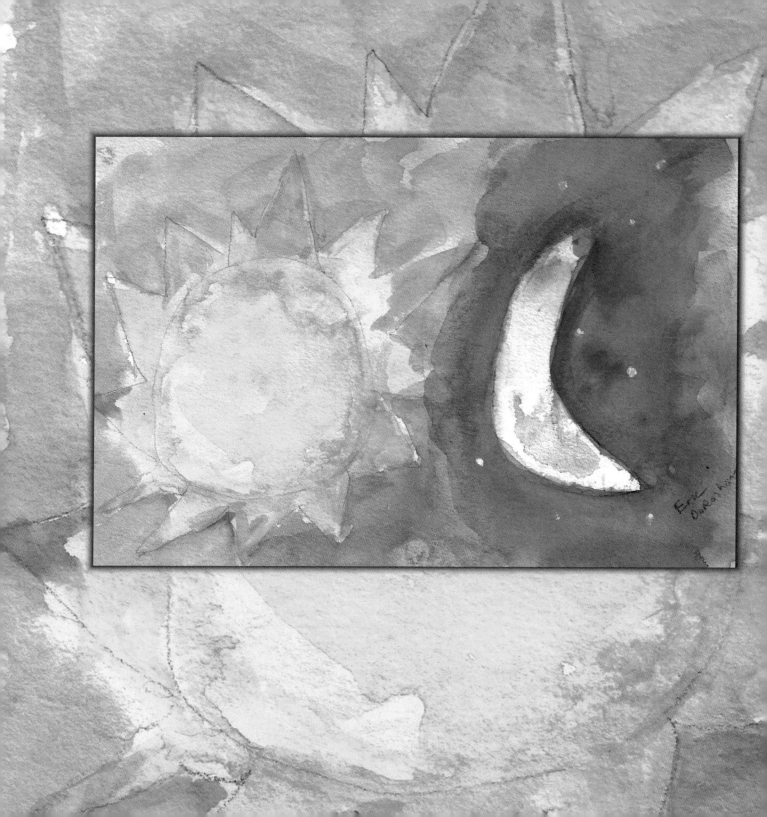

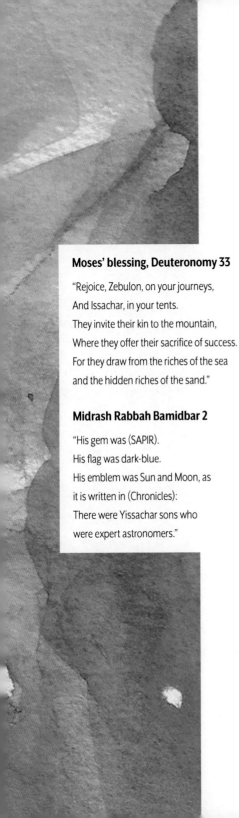

Moses' blessing, Deuteronomy 33

"Rejoice, Zebulon, on your journeys,
And Issachar, in your tents.
They invite their kin to the mountain,
Where they offer their sacrifice of success.
For they draw from the riches of the sea
and the hidden riches of the sand."

Midrash Rabbah Bamidbar 2

"His gem was (SAPIR).
His flag was dark-blue.
His emblem was Sun and Moon, as
it is written in (Chronicles):
There were Yissachar sons who
were expert astronomers."

THE TRIBE OF ISSACHAR

ISSACHAR WAS THE NINTH SON OF JACOB, AND THE FIFTH CHILD OF LEAH. THE TRIBE WAS BOUNDED ON THE NORTH BY ZEBULUN AND NAPHTALI AND ON THE EAST BY THE JORDAN RIVER. THE LAND WAS FERTILE AND A STRATEGIC KEY TO PALESTINE, HOWEVER, THE FLAT DEFENSELESS CHARACTER OF THE LAND AREA EXPOSED ISSACHAR TO INVASIONS.

It is written in the Aggadah that there was a strong relationship between the tribes of Issachar and Zebulun.

Zebulun was a merchant tribe, involved with the buying and selling of goods. It provided for its brother tribe so that Issachar could study Torah. This is hinted at in Deuteronomy 33:

"Rejoice, Zebulun, on your journeys,

And Issachar, in your tents."

The Tribe was known for its scholars. It produced

200 heads of the Sanhedrin (1 Chronicles 12:33).

In the Song of Deborah, Issachar was commended for participating in the war against Sisera. Deborah herself may have come from Issachar (Judges 5:15).

The territory of Issachar was eventually conquered by Assyria and annexed as a province. The tribe had expert astronomers. Their flag emblem had the sun and the moon in its center.

Picking up on those themes, my painting of the sun and moon with a dark blue background is my depiction of the tribe of Issachar.

NOTES

_____

_____

_____

_____

_____

_____

_____

_____

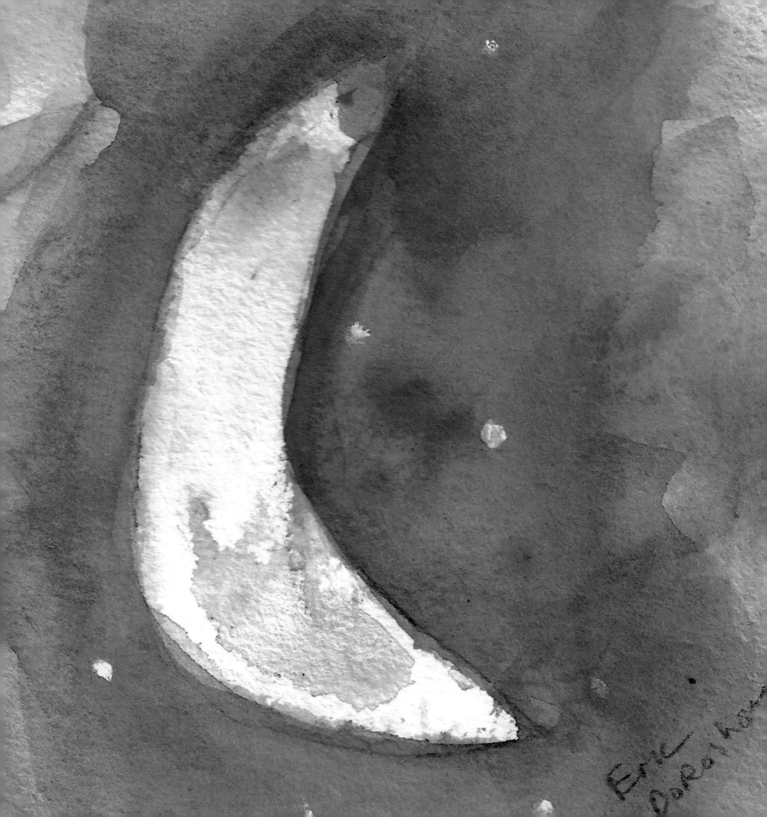

THE TRIBE OF JOSEPH

JOSEPH WAS THE FIRSTBORN OF RACHEL, JACOB'S BELOVED WIFE, AND WAS JACOB'S FAVORITE SON. JOSEPH RECEIVED LONG AND SOLEMN BLESSINGS FROM BOTH JACOB AND MOSES.

In Genesis, there is a well-known story about the jealousy of Joseph's brothers. There was a plot to kill him. He was sold to a caravan of merchants and sent to Egypt.

Joseph was sold into slavery, but he quickly earned the confidence of his master, who promoted him to oversee his estate (Genesis: 39). He went on to become the pharaoh's trusted advisor.

According to the *Encyclopedia Judaica,* Vol. 10, page 283 (1972 edition):

> *"The focus of attention on this Genesis narrative is the nobility of Joseph's character and the salvation that came through suffering, placing the incident in the concatenation of events that led eventually to the migration of the*

*Israelites to Egypt, their enslavement and redemption.
It was precisely as a result of Joseph's innocent suffering
that he was enabled to rise to power."*

The Aggadah also explores the extraordinary career of Joseph. His loyalty to his family, his conduct in high office with modesty and integrity, and his love of his father are consistent themes.

In Islam, the story of "Yusuf" tells that he was one of Muhammad's most beloved persons. In fact a whole sura, which contained one hundred and eleven continuous verses, was consecrated to him.

My painting theme is taken from the blessing of Jacob, as quoted on the previous page. A branch of a tree and grapes, growing on a wall near a stream, is portrayed in the watercolor as symbolic of the tribe of Joseph.

Because of his status, Joseph's two children had tribes: Ephraim and Manasseh.

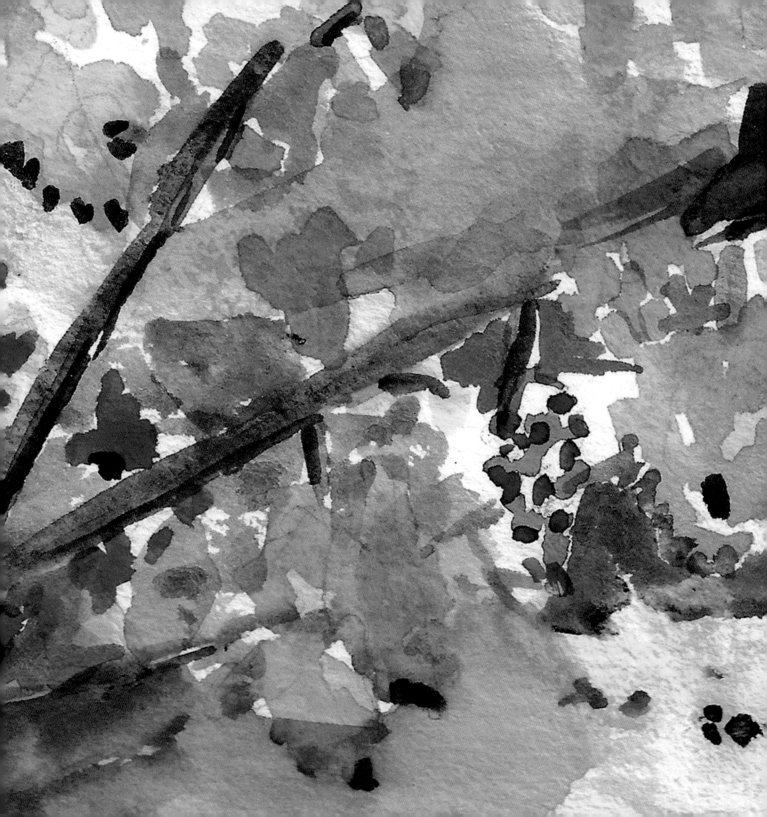

The Tribe of Ephraim

The tribe of Ephraim was the leading tribe in the central and northern parts of Israel. This tribe played a primary role in Jewish history and produced the majority of the kings of the Northern Kingdom.

Much of the area where the tribe settled was originally unpopulated; this actually protected the tribe from serious clashes with other inhabitants. The tribe had the strength to endure snow, hail, cold and heat (Psalms 80:3). Ephraim was granted precedence over its brother tribe Manasseh in the distribution of the Holy land (Joshua 16:5).

According to the Bible, the conquest of Canaan was led by Joshua of the Tribe of Ephraim. The religious center of Shiloh was located in this tribal area. The tribe claimed seniority over many of the other tribes, including its brother tribe, Manasseh, in military and political matters.

In the Song of Deborah (Judges 5:14), the tribe was praised for assisting in a military victory. According to *The Encyclopedia Judaica*, page 807 (1972

Edition):

> *"The self-aggrandizement of the Ephraimites over the other tribes and their tendency to isolation, inherent in such self-aggrandizement, ultimately proved fatal to themselves and to the entire nation, since it brought about the division in the kingdom of David and Solomon and the diminution of the state's prestige."*

The Tribe of Manasseh

The tribe of Manasseh occupied land contiguous to its brother tribe, Ephraim. There was a strong rivalry between the tribes, each striving for superiority over the other. In Joshua 17, the territory of the tribe is set out.

It is written that the inhabitants of the tribe had difficulty in expelling the Canaanites in the region.

NOTES

_____

_____

_____

_____

_____

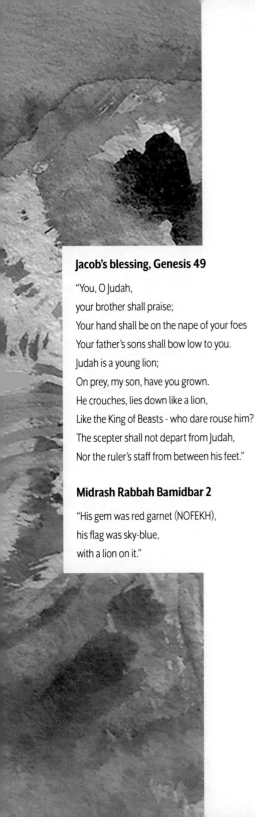

Jacob's blessing, Genesis 49

"You, O Judah,
your brother shall praise;
Your hand shall be on the nape of your foes
Your father's sons shall bow low to you.
Judah is a young lion;
On prey, my son, have you grown.
He crouches, lies down like a lion,
Like the King of Beasts - who dare rouse him?
The scepter shall not depart from Judah,
Nor the ruler's staff from between his feet."

Midrash Rabbah Bamidbar 2

"His gem was red garnet (NOFEKH),
his flag was sky-blue,
with a lion on it."

THE TRIBE OF JUDAH

JUDAH WAS THE FOURTH SON OF LEAH. HE REVEALED HIS LEADERSHIP BY PREVENTING THE KILLING OF JOSEPH BY HIS OTHER BROTHERS. BECAUSE OF THE SINS COMMITTED BY THE ELDER BROTHERS, JUDAH BECAME THE PRIVILEGED RECIPIENT OF MANY BLESSINGS.

The Tribe of Judah settled in the southern part of the Land of Israel. Judah was cut off from the rest of the tribes by a Canaanite land strip. The City of Jerusalem was at the heart of that territory and had the largest population of the tribes of Israel, numbering 74,600 (Numbers 1:27).

Initially, the tribe had a low status because many of its members were non-Israelites. However, the tribe acquired an important role based on its size and leadership. During the monarchy, tribal leadership duties passed to Judah. As a result, the tribe played a key role in the economic and political history of the 12 tribes. This is reflected

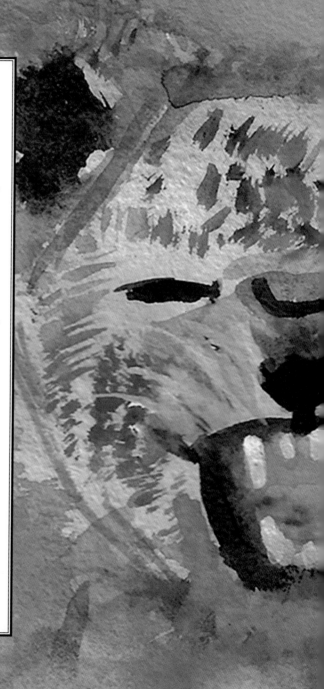

in the following quote from Genesis 49:10:

"The scepter shall not depart from Judah, or the ruler's staff from between his feet."

A rivalry formed between the tribes of Judah and Benjamin and this led in part to the battle of Gibeah. As a result of the defeat of the Benjamites, the Israelite opposition to the Philistine invaders was weakened.

The tribe had close ties with the tribe of Simeon.

As reported in the October 30, 2018 edition of *Haaretz*, new archeological analysis suggests the tribe worshiped Yahweh, as well as pagan idols. Dan competed with Judah as a center of worship.

This tribe produced many prominent leaders, including King David and his dynasty. In order to gain the favor of the notables of the tribe of Judah, David made gifts to them. He also protected tribe members from raiders in the desert, and they were grateful for these protections.

Further, his connections by marriage to many prominent Judean families helped cement his rapport with the tribe. The tribe tore itself lose from the dynasty of Saul and appointed David their king (II Samuel. 2:4). David united the tribes and made Jerusalem its capital. After his death, Palestine was divided into two kingdoms: Israel in the north and Judah in the south.

In my watercolor, the tribe of Judah is portrayed as a young lion as reflected in Jacob's blessing. The Midrash indicates that the gem color of the tribe was red and the color of the flag was blue, both of which are in the watercolor.

NOTES _____
_____
_____
_____
_____
_____
_____
_____
_____
_____
_____
_____

Jacob's blessing, Genesis 49

"Cursed be their anger so fierce,
And their wrath so relentless.
I will divide them in Jacob
Scatter them in Israel."

Moses' blessing, Deuteronomy 33

"And kept Your covenant.
They shall teach Your laws to Jacob,
Your norms to Israel.
They shall offer You incense to savor,
And whole-burnt offering on Your altar.
Bless, O Lord, his substance,
And favor his undertakings.
Smite the loins of his foes;
Let his enemies rise no more."

THE TRIBE OF LEVI

LEVI WAS THE THIRD SON OF LEAH AND JACOB. MOSES, HIS BROTHER AARON, THE HIGH PRIEST, AND THEIR SISTER MIRIAM, THE PROPHETESS, WERE LEVITES. LEVI WAS SIMEON'S PARTNER IN THE MASSACRE AT SHECHEM.

Levi was the smallest tribe and had a strong connection to the tribe of Judah.

During the "Golden Calf" episode, Moses called upon everybody who remained faithful to assist him in punishing the transgressors. The entire Levi tribe came to him, signifying that there was no sinner among them. Thus, the Levites showed their loyalty to Moses. They were ready to disregard the other tribes when called to fight the idol worshipers. They killed some 3,000 people (Exodus 32:38).

As a reward for their faithfulness, the tribe of Levi was appointed to serve the Priests in religious matters in the Sanctuary. Their duties included providing a barrier between the tabernacle and the people. The tribe members were overseers of the House of the Lord, as well as singers, musicians, gatekeepers and guardians. They also functioned as officials, judges and craftsmen for the Temple service, supervisors of the chambers and the courts, and overseers of the Temple treasury. They were in charge of the royal service (I Chronicles 9) and received a tithe for their service (Numbers 18:21).

The tribe was involved in the transfer of the monarchy to David. They were firm supporters of the dynasty of David until the destruction of the Temple.

The Levites did not own land, but settled in towns and areas set aside for them within other tribes' territories (Joshua 21). Thus, Jacob's prophecy was fulfilled.

In my painting, I used yellow to be symbolic of divine light. The candles are symbolic of the important religious functions that the tribe performed.

NOTES

Jacob's blessing, Genesis 49

"Naphtali is a hind let loose,
Which yields lovely fawns."

Moses' blessing, Deuteronomy 33

"Oh Naphtali, sated with favor
And full of LORD's blessings,
Take possession on the west and south."

Midrash Rabbah Bamidbar 2

"His gem was amethyst (AKHLAMA),
his color was like clear wine, some
mild redness.
His emblem was a free hind."

THE TRIBE OF NAPHTALI

NAPHTALI WAS A FULL BROTHER TO DAN AND THE SECOND SON OF BILAH, RACHAEL'S SERVANT. THIS SMALL TRIBE SETTLED IN THE NORTH LAND OF ISRAEL AND WAS CONSIDERED TO BE OF INFERIOR STATUS.

Yet, the tribe had importance from an agricultural and military standpoint (Deuteronomy 33:22 and Joshua 19:35). The designation of the whole of Galilee as "the land of Naphtali" (II Kings 15:29) shows the importance of this tribe among the other northern tribes.

Naphtali played an important role in the defeat of the Canaanites during the time of Deborah (Judges 4:6). The men of the tribe, led by Barak, risked their lives on the heights of the field (Judges 5:18).

In the time of David, the tribe became a royal administrative district that had both religious and administrative functions. Dan was likely absorbed into the tribe of Naphtali (I Kings 15:20). There were three Levitical cities in Naphtali: Kedesh in the Galilee, which was a city of refuge for manslayers, Hammoth-Dor and Kartan (Joshua 21:32).

In my watercolor, I painted a hind (a deer), which is mentioned in Jacob's blessing. The red wine color suggested in the Midrash surrounds the deer in the painting.

NOTES

_____

_____

_____

_____

_____

_____

_____

_____

_____

_____

_____

_____

_____

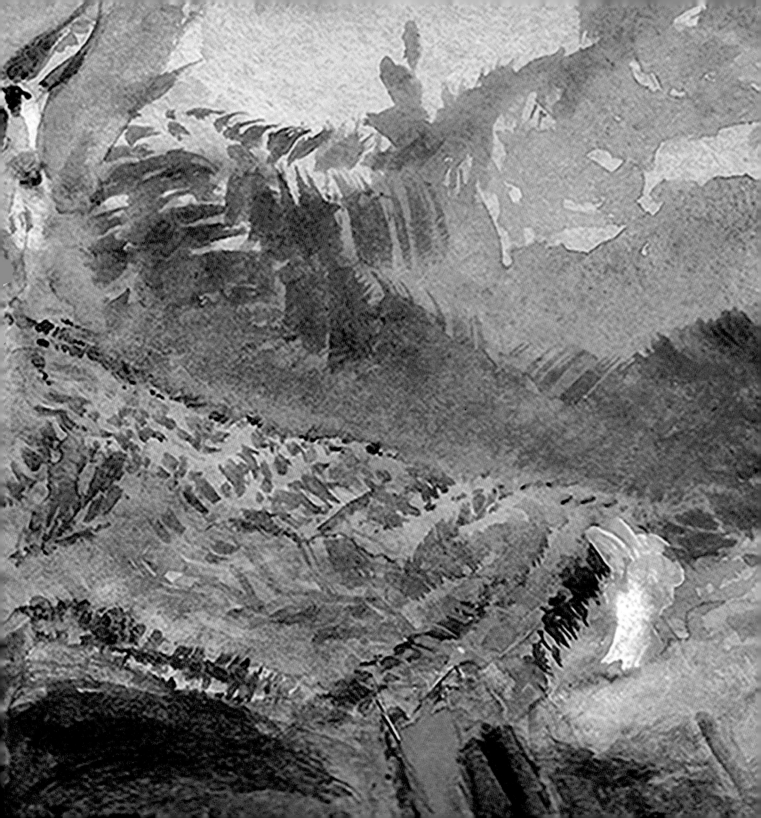

Jacob's blessing, Genesis 49

"Reuben, you are my first-born.
My might and first fruit of my vigor;
Exceeding in rank
and exceeding in honor
Unstable as water,
you shall excel no longer."

Moses' blessing, Deuteronom 33

"May Reuben live and not die
Though few be his numbers."

Midrash Rabbah Bamidbar 2

"His gem was a Ruby (ODEM),
his flag was red.
It had an image of a mandragore."

THE TRIBE OF REUBEN

REUBEN WAS THE ELDEST SON OF JACOB AND LEAH AND WAS CONSIDERED GENEROUS BUT HOT TEMPERED. REUBEN DISAPPOINTED HIS FATHER IN HIS PERSONAL BEHAVIOR. THEREFORE, JACOB DISCONTINUED REUBEN'S SPECIAL STATUS AS THE ELDEST AND THE SPECIAL "FIRSTBORN'S RIGHT" TO A DOUBLE SHARE IN THE HERITAGE. INSTEAD, THIS WAS GIVEN TO JOSEPH.

Initially, the tribe of Reuben had an important position as the head of the tribal league. Later, after the conquest of land, the tribe played no special role in ancient Israeli history. Just before the entry to the Land of Israel, Reubenites, together with the tribe of Gad, approached Moses and asked him to grant them the Transjordanian territories. Moses granted the request as long as the tribe served as Israel's vanguard in capturing western Palestine. Only after the tribe had kept its agreement was it given permission to return east. The tribe built an altar near the Jordan River as proof that the tribes on the east bank were an important part of Israel (Joshua 22:10).

The tribe was semi-nomadic, subsisting on raising sheep. Deborah berated Reuben for not participating in the war against Jabin and Sisera. The tribe chose to "tarry among the sheepfolds, to hear the piping for the flocks" (Judges 5:15-16).

At one time, Reuben was near extinction. In Deuteronomy 33:6, there is prayer for its survival. The tribe became weak and was gradually absorbed by the tribe of Gad. It retained some identity until the territory was annexed and its inhabitants were exiled by Assyria (I Chronicles 5:6).

My watercolor is of a mandragore plant (also known as mandrake), which is mentioned in the Midrash as being on its flag. The plant is native to the Mediterranean region and has thick upright roots. Red is in the painting, reflecting the tribe's red flag as suggested in the Midrash.

NOTES
_____
_____
_____
_____
_____
_____
_____
_____
_____
_____
_____
_____
_____
_____
_____
_____
_____
_____
_____
_____
_____
_____
_____

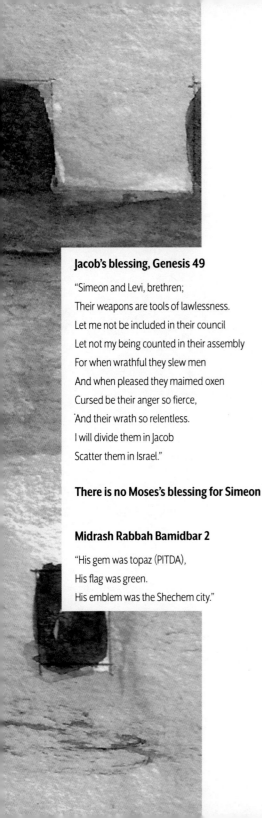

Jacob's blessing, Genesis 49

"Simeon and Levi, brethren;
Their weapons are tools of lawlessness.
Let me not be included in their council
Let not my being counted in their assembly
For when wrathful they slew men
And when pleased they maimed oxen
Cursed be their anger so fierce,
And their wrath so relentless.
I will divide them in Jacob
Scatter them in Israel."

There is no Moses's blessing for Simeon

Midrash Rabbah Bamidbar 2

"His gem was topaz (PITDA),
His flag was green.
His emblem was the Shechem city."

THE TRIBE OF SIMEON

SIMEON WAS THE SECOND SON OF JACOB. HE WAS CHARACTERIZED BY HIS ZEAL AND EXTREMISM. SIMEON, WITH HIS PARTNER, LEVI, TOOK REVENGE ON THE CITY OF SHECHEM BY KILLING ALL OF THE MALES, CAPTURING THE WOMEN AND CHILDREN AND ALL OF THE LIVESTOCK. THE MASSACRE WAS IN RETALIATION FOR THE RAPE OF THEIR SISTER, DINAH, BY SHECHEM, WHO WAS A PRINCE IN THE LAND (GENESIS 34).

After the People of Israel came into the promised land, the tribe of Simeon failed to conquer the area allotted to it. Therefore, the tribe of Judah invited Simeon to settle within the Judea area, and eventually Judea absorbed Simeon. Thus, Simeon's territory was referred to as *The Negev of Judah*.

Joshua gathered all of the tribes to Simeon when the tribes entered into a covenant to worship the Lord (Joshua 24). However, no members of the tribe enjoyed an important position in the organization of the 12 tribes. No judges were appointed from the tribe.

The tribe of Simeon engaged in a pastoral, semi-nomadic life in the Negev, with members of the tribe grazing livestock in the southern part. The tribe suffered hardships from the desert climate and from fighting off-border tribes.

The tribe of Simeon virtually disappeared during the early monarchy. Its fate was tied to the tribe of Judah. There is no mention at all of Simeon in The Song of Deborah (Judges 5).

According to the Midrash, the tribe's flag had an emblem of the City of Shechem, which was victimized by the Simeon brother. In my watercolor, I painted a castle, which is symbolic of the city. The green color of the tribe as suggested in the Midrash is shown in the entrance of the castle.

NOTES

Moses' blessing, Deuteronomy 33

'Rejoice, Zebulon, on your journeys,
And Issachar, in your tents.
They invite their kin to the mountain,
Where they offer their sacrifice of success.
For they draw from the riches of the sea
And the hidden riches of the sand."

Midrash Rabbah Bamidbar 2

"His gem was a diamond (YAHALOM).
This flag was white with a ship drawn on it,
as it is written:
Zebulon will dwell at the sea shore."

THE TRIBE OF ZEBULUN

ZEBULUN WAS THE 10TH SON OF JACOB.
ISSACHAR AND ZEBULUN WERE THE TWO
YOUNGEST CHILDREN OF LEAH, AND THE
TWO ARE JOINED TOGETHER IN MOSES' BLESS-
INGS. THE BROTHERS DECIDED THAT ISSACHAR
WOULD DEDICATE HIMSELF TO THE STUDY
OF THE TORAH AND THAT ZEBULUN WOULD
PROVIDE FOR HIM. THIS IS HINTED AT IN THE
ABOVE BLESSING OF MOSES.

The tribe had a major position among the tribes
of Galilee. Zebulun was predicted to have a mar-
itime vocation. The tribe occupied a small yet
fertile territory in the Lower Galilee, which was
crossed by active commercial routes and had ports,
including Zidon (currently located in Lebanon).
Zebulun was active in the campaigns of the period
of the Judges. Deborah praised them as a "people
that put its life in jeopardy to the point of death"
(Judges 5:18).

During the period of the United Kingdom, the tribe of Zebulun maintained the largest army of the western tribes, which fought under King David (I Chronicles 12:34). The tribe traveled to Jerusalem to celebrate Hezekiah's Passover (II Chronicles 30:10-11). He was a king of Judah.

Zebulun suffered less than other regions during the destruction of the Kingdom of Israel. Apparently, the tribe was not uprooted and survived the Assyrian campaign in the Galilee (II Chronicles 30:6).

The populous Jewish community in the Galilee, in the period of the Second Temple, in all likelihood was a remnant of the tribe of Zebulun. Rabbinic legends reflect that the tribe and its descendants were generous in supporting institutions of learning.

My painting of the tribe is a sunset on the water with a sailing ship on the right of the painting. This nautical scene is symbolic of the tribe as suggested in the blessings of Moses.

NOTES

_____

_____

_____

_____

_____

_____

_____

_____

_____

_____

_____

_____

_____

_____

_____

_____

_____

_____

_____

_____

_____

_____

How the challenges that the 12 Tribes faced are relevant to us today

THE STORY OF THE 12 TRIBES OF ISRAEL IS FUN-
DAMENTAL AND FOUNDATIONAL IN THE JEWISH
RELIGION. EVEN TODAY, THE STORY OF THE
12 TRIBES PROVIDES IMPORTANT LESSONS FOR
PEOPLE OF ALL FAITHS. BUT HOW WERE THEIR
CHALLENGES RELEVANT TO US? WHAT LESSONS
CAN WE LEARN FROM THEIR STRUGGLES?

The War of Deborah Shows the Importance of Strong Female Leadership

The War of Deborah demonstrated the positive
effects of a strong female leadership. The Song of
Deborah, which described the war of Deborah and
her victory, is one of the earliest Hebrew heroic
poems and is found in Judges 5:2-31. It is a victory hymn and song about the defeat of Canaanite

adversaries by several tribes, led by Deborah.

Deborah was a judge. She sat under a palm tree and dispensed justice in the open air. She was a strong woman and considered to be a national leader of Israel in a time before Israel had a king. She was considered the mother of Israel (Judges 5:7), and she promoted a war of liberation against the oppressive King Jabin of Canaan and his general, Sisera, who had ruthlessly oppressed Israel for 20 years.

Deborah appointed Barak as her general. Sisera was well armed with 900 chariots (Judges 4:3), but Israel did not possess any chariots (Judges: 4:3).

Barak's army of 10,000 men from the tribes of Naphtali and Zebulun climbed Mount Tabor, located in the lower Galilee. Sisera's army was in the Kishon River valley, where there was flooding at that time. Deborah ordered Barak to exploit the flooding, move down from Mount Tabor and storm Sisera's camp.

The battle was joined. Sisera's chariots sank deep into the river bed mire and were disabled. The

Israelite army put Sisera's entire camp to the sword.

Sisera fled and the story of a second strong woman is told. Jael came in contact with a fleeing Sisera and killed him, crushing his head with a hammer (Judges 5:25).

According to the *Encyclopedic Judaica*, the victory *"marked the permanent decline of the Canaanite kingdom and ushered in a period of 40 years of tranquility of Israel."* The Song of Deborah is therefore very important, for it celebrates a military victory led by two women: Deborah and Jael.

The Importance of Working Together to Reach a Common Goal

The story of the 12 Tribes of Israel in the Bible is replete with narratives about the importance of teamwork. Joshua was appointed by Moses to be his successor, to conquer the land of Canaan and to apportion the land among the tribes. He was from the tribe of Ephraim. Initially, the tribes were united under Joshua's leadership and were successful in their military conquests of many cities. However, later mopping up operations were left to several of the individual tribes.

The narrative of two tribes working together for a peaceful means to an end is discussed in the Aggadah. Zebulun was a merchant tribe that bought and sold goods and thereby provided for the tribe Issachar. This then enabled Issachar to study Torah. As a result, the tribe of Issachar produced 200 heads of the Sanhedrin[1] (I Chronicles 12:33).

In the Book of Samuel, the story of the tribes working to defeat another evil king is told in I Samuel: 11. Nahash, who was the king of the Ammonites, was an attacker of the Jewish tribes, especially the descendants of Gad and Ruben. His population surrender terms consisted of either death or having their right eyes gouged out.

There was an appeal for help from their fellow Israelite tribes, and Saul, who was later to become king, showed his leadership talents by issuing a call to the tribes to rally around him. He took a yoke

---

1 The Sanhedrin was an assembly of rabbis appointed to sit in a tribunal in ancient Israel.

of oxen and cut it into pieces, which he sent by messengers throughout the tribes with a warning: "Thus shall be done to the cattle of anyone who does not follow Saul and Samuel into battle" (I Samuel 11:7).

Saul's force, which consisted of 30,000 soldiers from the tribe of Judah and 300,000 soldiers from the other tribes, inflicted a stunning defeat on the Ammonites. This victory helped pave the way for Saul to be Israel's first king.

NOTES

_____

_____

_____

_____

_____

_____

_____

_____

_____

_____

SEVERAL BASIC CONCEPTS OF OUR CIVIL LAW TODAY ARE REFLECTED IN THE LAWS GIVEN TO THE 10 TRIBES

A Woman's Right to Inherit and Own Property

As told in the Bible, a man named Zelophehad from the Tribe of Manasseh died in the wilderness without a male issue (Numbers 26:33). His five daughters came forward and requested from Moses that they be recognized as female heirs and be granted their father's inheritance. The daughters argued that their father committed no sin that might merit the destruction of his name.

Moses brought their case before the Lord and the Lord upheld the plea of the daughters. Moses was then told to speak to the Israelite people to make clear that if a man dies without leaving a son, his property shall go to his daughters Numbers 27:8.

In the Aggadah, the daughters are highly praised for their sagacity in presenting their problem at an appropriate time and in their clear ability to argue their own case.

The idea that women could own property in their own right was very far ahead of its time. It was not until the passage of the Married Women's Property Acts beginning in 1839 that women could legally own property in the United States. Delaware gave no legal status to women until late in the nineteenth century.

The Forgiveness of Debt

In Deuteronomy, chapter 1, Moses addressed all of the tribes of Israel about the instructions God had given him before they crossed the Jordan River. Every seventh year, the members of the 12 tribes were told to practice remission of debts, and dunning was strictly prohibited (Deuteronomy 15:1-2). This legal precept presaged our modern day bankruptcy law, which gives many debtors a discharge of their debts every eight years.

Ethical Rules for Judges

In Deuteronomy 16:18, magistrates and officials for the tribes were appointed. They were required to govern fairly and show no partiality. Bribes were strictly prohibited. "Justice, justice shall you pursue" was their mandate (Deuteronomy 16:20). The same concepts of justice and fairness of judges are embedded in the court system in the United States.

The Rules of Legal Responsibility Toward Others

In the Torah, Moses is regarded as the ideal of "strict and unbending justice." *Encyclopedia Judaica*, page 478 (1972 Edition). The concepts of justice, fairness, responsibility and equality are constant themes in the story of the 12 tribes.

In his book *Everyday Holiness* by Alan Morinis, the author writes on page 206 that Jewish law requires that one who sees lost property is fully obligated to divest himself of the property and assist in its return. This concept originates from Deuteronomy 22:1-3 where the Israelite tribes were required to return an ox or sheep going astray and not ignore this obligation. This precept is based on a worldview that dictates our responsibility to our brethren. This fundamental concept of responsibility to return the property of others is embedded in laws of our civil and criminal judicial system in the United States.

Additionally, the modern-day legal requirement to pay fair compensation in our civil justice system can find it roots in the in the story of the 12 tribes. In Exodus 21:18-19, a compensation system is established to pay a victim for lost wages resulting from injuries sustained from an unjustified non fatal assault. The Rabbis of the Talmud[1] interpreted this section to also permit compensation for the pain the victim suffered as well as the shame he incurred from his injuries. The victim was to be "thoroughly healed," which the Rabbis in the Talmud interpret as requiring the payment of the victim's doctor's bills.

Further, the "eye for an eye, tooth for a tooth" precept in Leviticus 24:18-20 has been interpreted by the Rabbis as not requiring retaliation against

---

[1] The Talmud is a compilation of the writings of historic rabbis discussing and debating what the Torah means.

the perpetrator. For them, the real meaning of the phrase is the expression of justice and equality. Therefore, a person at fault in causing a personal injury must pay adequate and equitable compensation, after a fair judicial review of the matter.

The Concept of Equal Justice Under Law

In Leviticus 24:22, it is commanded that only one "manner of law" was to be used for both the "stranger" and for the "home-born". This precept established the concept of legal equality between the alien and native. This is lauded as one of the great texts of Scripture and is considered the basis for the brotherhood of man. This precept finds direct application in today's American judicial system. The concept of the equal application of the law is venerated in the American Court system. The phrase "equal justice under law "is engraved in the front of the United State Supreme Court building in Washington DC. The words are derived from the 14th Amendment to the U.S. Constitution which states that no state shall "deny to any person within its jurisdiction the equal protection of the laws."

In Conclusion

David McCullough wrote in his book *Brave Companions Portraits in History*:

> *"How can we know who we are and where we are going if we don't anything about where we have come from and what we have been through, the courage shown, the costs paid, to be where we are?"*

I hope that the paintings, along with the information in this book, give you pleasure, comfort and guidance as you face life's unprecedented challenges.

~ Eric Doroshow

Photo courtesy of Eric Doroshow

Photo courtesy of Eric Doroshow

Photo courtesy of Eric Doroshow

About the Author & Artist

Eric M. Doroshow is an attorney, artist, author, and life coach. He is in a private law practice in Delaware. He started his law practice in 1978 with one office and one client. Since that time, his firm has become the 11th largest law firm in the State of Delaware, with eight offices throughout the State.

His practice focuses on representing consumers in their claims against insurance companies. Additionally, he represents consumers and small business persons in Bankruptcy Court.

He has been a frequent lecturer on legal matters for The Delaware State Bar Association, The Delaware Trial Lawyers Association, as well as consumer groups throughout Delaware.

He began painting at the age of 50. He has no formal artistic training, except for taking classes in watercolor and acrylics with well-known artists in Delaware.

He was a history major in college. After college, he developed a keen interest in Jewish historical themes. This is his first published book.

Acknowledgments

This project would not have been completed without the help of several people. I would like to thank Wendy Hatch, Ellen Rice, Chris Thackray and my wife Aida. Wendy is a professional artist in Wilmington, Delaware and is my teacher at the Delaware Art Museum. Her support and guidance were critical to me as I painted the 12 watercolors. Ellen Rice is a professional artist with a gallery in Ocean View, Delaware. She helped turn the 12 watercolors into an attractive giclée print. Ellen, Chris, along with my wife Aida, also helped with the editing of this book.

The 12 Tribes of Israel

Asher

Benjamin

Dan

Gad

Yssachar

Joseph

Judah

Levi

Naphtali

Reuben

Simeon

Zebulun

How to Order Prints and Books

Signed archival prints of the 12 Tribes of Israel are available in two sizes: 8"x10" and 16"x20" for easy framing. A high end giclée printing process was used to achieve an excellent color and detail reproduction of the 12 original water colors. Heavy weight paper was used for each print for long term durability and a radiant look and feel for each print.

Eric can be reached by email at EricDoroshow@ dplaw.com. Or by phone at 302-998-0100.

To Order Prints or Additional Copies
of this book, go to:

www.imagesinspired.net

All proceeds to be donated to Jewish charities.*

---

* Purchases of art and booklet may not be eligible for a charitable contribution. Consult your tax advisor.